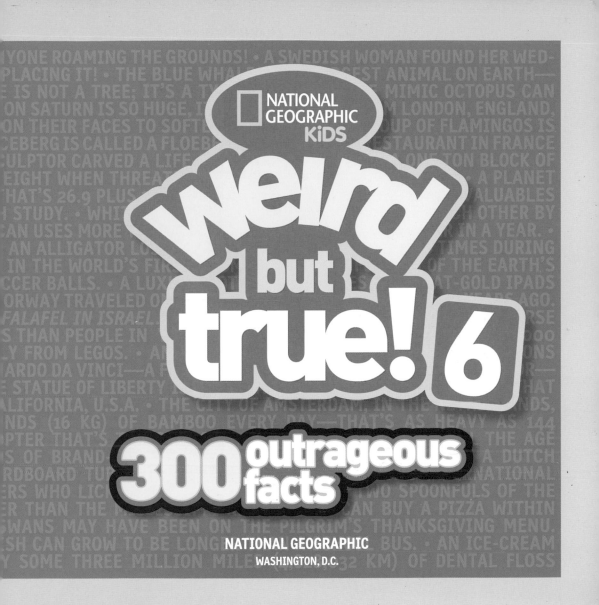

Visit us online:
Kids: kids.nationalgeographic.com
Parents: nationalgeographic.com
Teachers: nationalgeographic.com/education
Librarians: ngchildrensbooks.org

For information about special discounts for
bulk purchases, please contact National
Geographic Books Special Sales:
ngspecsales@ngs.org

For rights or permissions inquiries,
please contact National Geographic
Books Subsidiary Rights:
ngbookrights@ngs.org

Paperback ISBN: 978-1-4263-1490-2
Reinforced Library Binding
   ISBN: 978-1-4263-1491-9

Printed in China
14/PPS/1

AN EMPEROR PENGUIN HAS 100 FEATHERS PER SQUARE INCH (6.5 square cm) OF ITS BODY.

THE ASIAN WEAVER ANT

CAN HOLD OBJECTS **100 TIMES** ITS WEIGHT— WHILE HANGING ¡NMOᗡ ƎᗡISᑫU

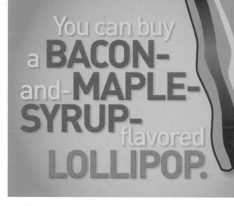

You can buy a **BACON-** and-**MAPLE-SYRUP-** flavored **LOLLIPOP.**

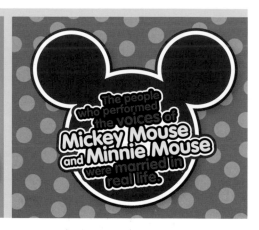

The people who performed the voices of **Mickey Mouse** and **Minnie Mouse** were married in real life.

A STUDY FOUND THAT **HOT CHOCOLATE** TASTES SWEETER WHEN YOU DRINK IT FROM

AN **ORANGE** CUP VS. A **WHITE** CUP.

Kool-Aid can be used to clean dishwashers.

The **ears** of the **long-eared** **jerboa,** a nocturnal **rodent,** are two-thirds the size of **its body.**

THERE'S A

FUNGUS
THAT SECRETES
RED DROPS

THAT LOOK LIKE

BLOOD.

YOUR FINGERPRINT. YOUR IRIS—THE COLORED PART OF YOUR EYE—IS AS UNIQUE AS YOUR FINGERPRINT.

BEFORE THE DWARF PLANET MAKEMAKE WAS OFFICIALLY NAMED, SCIENTISTS CALLED IT "EASTERBUNNY."

PANDAS eat

AS MUCH AS

36 pounds
(16 kg)

OF

bamboo
every
day—

THAT'S AS HEAVY AS

144 hamburgers!

THE **WORLD'S** LARGEST WIND TURBINE HAS BLADES THE SIZE OF A **COMMERCIAL JET.**

SOME ANCIENT ROMANS RUBBED **CROCODILE DUNG** ON THEIR FACES TO SOFTEN THEIR SKIN.

Hatshepsut, the first female **pharaoh** *of Egypt, wore red and* **black** *nail polish.*

A group of flamingos is called a **flamboyance.**

For 213 years it was **illegal for women to wear pants in Paris**— luckily the law was never really enforced.

You'll never see a full moon and the sun in the sky at the same time.

THE JUICE OF **ONE** TYPE OF **CHILI PEPPER** CAN **BURN** THROUGH A **LATEX GLOVE.**

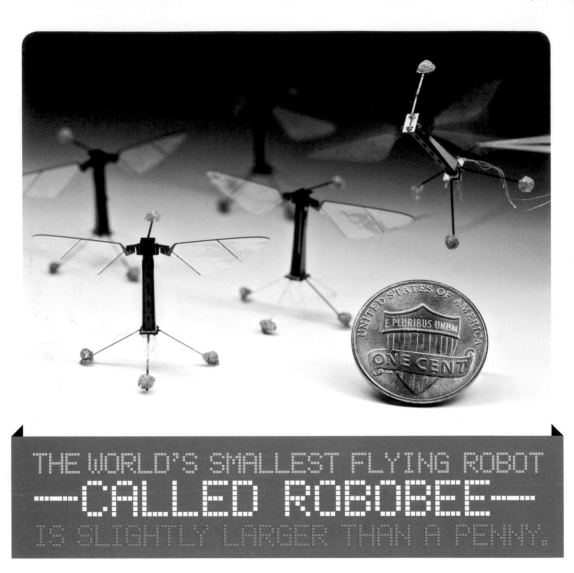

THE WORLD'S SMALLEST FLYING ROBOT
—CALLED ROBOBEE—
IS SLIGHTLY LARGER THAN A PENNY.

1.9 BILLION YEARS AGO, MUCH OF THE EARTH SMELLED LIKE ROTTEN EGGS.

The **Goliath spider's fangs** are as long as a **paper clip.**

THE **SHINIEST** LIVING THING ON EARTH

IS AN **AFRICAN FRUIT** KNOWN AS *POLLIA CONDENSATA.*

Male blue-footed **boobies** do a **high-step strut** to attract mates.

A **planet** partially made of **diamond** was calculated to be worth **$26.9 nonillion** (that's 26.9 plus 29 zeros)!

FOR
$100,000,
YOU CAN BUY A
KILLER WHALE-
SHAPED
SUBMARINE.

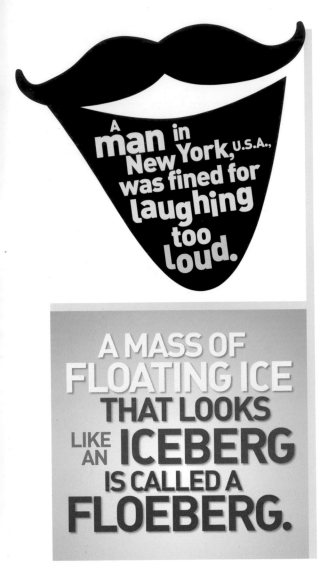

A **man** in **New York**, U.S.A., was fined for **laughing** **too** **loud**.

A MASS OF **FLOATING ICE** THAT LOOKS LIKE AN **ICEBERG** IS CALLED A **FLOEBERG.**

IF YOU **ROLLED ALL THE WATER ON EARTH INTO A BALL,** IT WOULD BE LESS THAN A THIRD THE SIZE OF THE MOON.

EARTH

MOON

WATER ON EARTH

The Indian giant squirrel has purple fur.

SOME **DOGS** ARE *ALLERGIC* TO **CATS.**

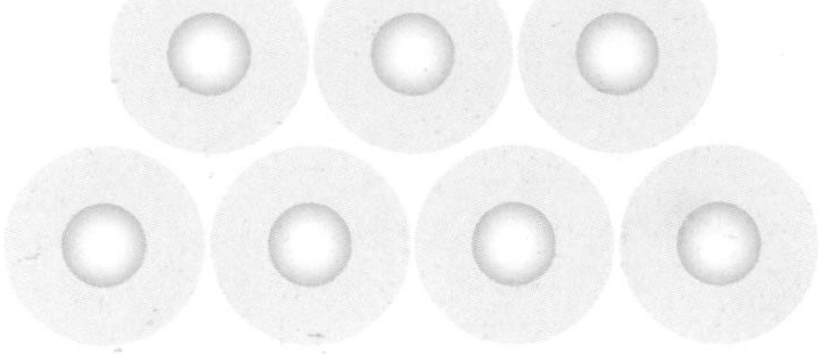

The world's largest
toilet-paper pyramid
was made up of
23,821 rolls.

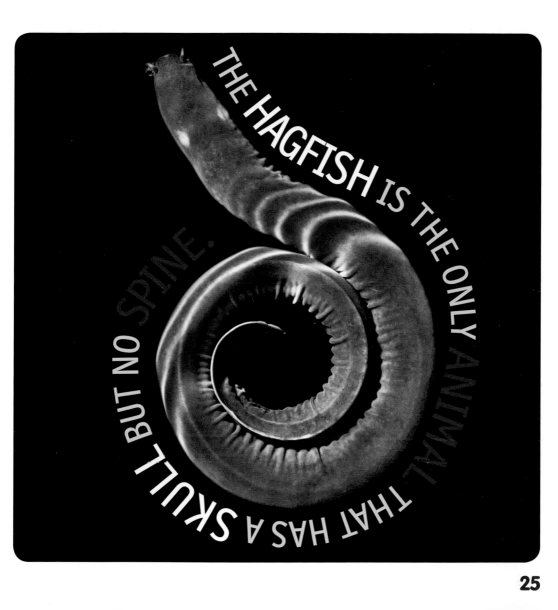

THE HAGFISH IS THE ONLY ANIMAL THAT HAS A SKULL BUT NO SPINE.

A PET **RABBIT** IN ENGLAND **WEIGHS** THE SAME AS **FOUR** BOWLING BALLS.

A WOMAN ONCE DISLOCATED HER JAW WHILE EATING A **GIANT** HAMBURGER.

Sunlight **reflected** off a building in London, England, **melted** a nearby car.

A RARE TYPE OF OCTOPUS HAS SIX ARMS.

IT CAN TAKE
TEN YEARS
FOR A
SAGUARO
CACTUS
TO GROW
AN **INCH** (2.5 CM).

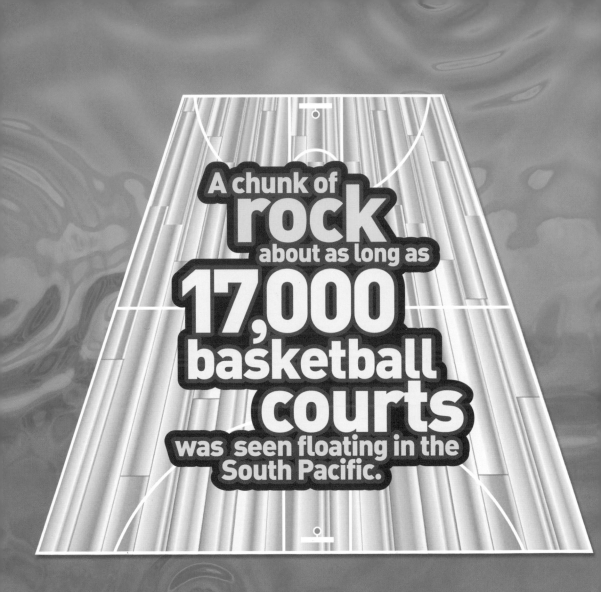

A chunk of **rock** about as long as **17,000** **basketball** **courts** was seen floating in the South Pacific.

Ghost ants have SEE-THROUGH STOMACHS.

A PIECE OF **CAKE** FROM **QUEEN VICTORIA'S** *wedding* HAS BEEN PRESERVED IN **ENGLAND FOR 174 YEARS.**

A company invented a remote-controlled helicopter that's the size of a golf ball.

KOMODO DRAGONS OFTEN VOMIT WHEN THREATENED.

SOME PLANTS **GLOW** BRIGHT BLUE UNDER ULTRAVIOLET LIGHT.

MORE THAN **HALF** THE **WORLD'S GEYSERS** ARE IN YELLOWSTONE NATIONAL **PARK** IN WYOMING, U.S.A.

THE NIGHT SIDE OF PLANET EARTH IS 600,000 TIMES DIMMER THAN ITS DAY SIDE.

The largest **kangaroos** can weigh as much as **grown men.**

NASA IS DEVELOPING A **3-D PRINTER** THAT IT HOPES WILL **PRINT EDIBLE PIZZAS.**

A **rare disorder** causes people **to sleep** for up to **20 hours** a day.

AT A STORE **IN JAPAN,** YOU CAN HAVE A REPLICA OF YOUR **FACE** MOLDED INTO **CHOCOLATE.**

The **bee hummingbird** snacks on up to **1,500 flowers** a day.

A SCULPTOR CARVED A **LIFE-SIZE ASTRONAUT** FROM A **ONE-TON BLOCK OF CHEDDAR CHEESE.**

AN ASTRONAUT WROTE HIS DAUGHTER'S INITIALS ON THE DUSTY SURFACE OF THE MOON.

Some frogs eat crabs.

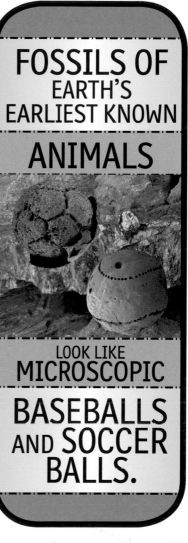

FOSSILS OF EARTH'S EARLIEST KNOWN ANIMALS LOOK LIKE MICROSCOPIC BASEBALLS AND SOCCER BALLS.

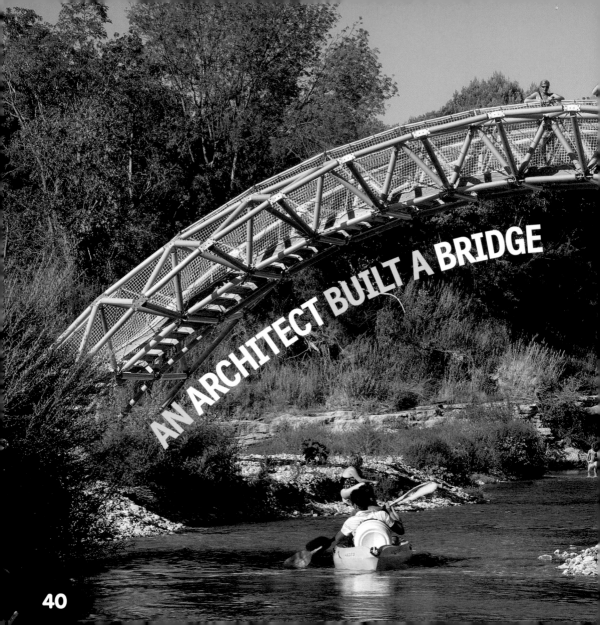

AN ARCHITECT BUILT A BRIDGE

OUT OF CARDBOARD TUBES.

THE **PIRATE ANT** IS NAMED FOR THE **BLACK PATCHES** ON ITS EYES.

Some **catfish leap** out of the **water** to catch **pigeons** on the shore.

Female **fireflies** rarely **fly.**

People **throw away** *enough* **ribbon** *each year to* **tie a bow** *around the entire* **Earth.**

Americans eat over a billion chicken wings during **Super Bowl** weekend.

About one out of **five people** have dropped their cell phone into the **toilet.**

A LEGO SCULPTURE OF ENGLAND'S QUEEN ELIZABETH II INCLUDED A CROWN WITH REAL DIAMONDS.

Borborygmus

is the word for the **rumbling sound** in your **stomach** when you're **hungry.**

Louis XIV of *France* wore *four-inch-high heels.* (10 cm)

The gray **catbird** makes a **meow** sound.

200 million Girl Scout **cookies** are sold every year— enough for each person in the U.S. to have half a box.

Some green snakes turn blue when they die.

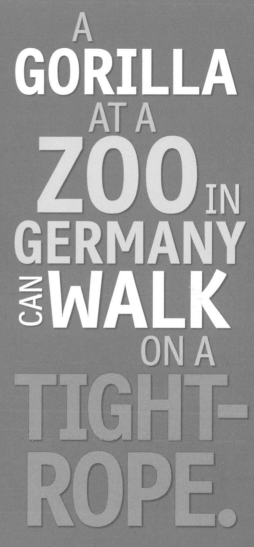

A **GORILLA** AT A **ZOO** IN **GERMANY** CAN **WALK** ON A **TIGHT-ROPE.**

Earthquakes can instantly create **gold** in Earth's crust.

An **avocado** is sometimes known as an **alligator pear.**

More people hide their **valuables** in their **sock drawer** than anywhere else, according to a British study.

A **SIX-CLAWED** LOBSTER WAS CAUGHT

COUNT THEM UP!

OFF THE COAST OF **MASSACHUSETTS,** U.S.A.

Wild strawberries can be yellow.

THERE'S A TOWN IN CANADA CALLED SAINT-LOUIS-DU-HA!-HA!

A WOOD FROG'S CROAK SOUNDS LIKE A QUACK.

SOME GRASSHOPPERS ARE PINK.

Scientists found that you can literally get **cold feet** when you're nervous.

IN ANCIENT GREECE, COMETS WERE CALLED "HAIRY STARS."

Some **house ants** smell like **fresh coconuts** when *smashed.*

A **woman in Sweden** found her **wedding ring** on a **carrot** growing in her garden—16 years after misplacing it!

27 feet (8 meters)

SUNFLOWERS CAN GROW AS TALL AS TWO AFRICAN ELEPHANTS STACKED UP.

The movie *Cloudy with a Chance of Meatballs* is called *Rain of Falafel* in Israel.

A disorder called **Alien Hand Syndrome** can cause a person to **punch** and **slap himself.**

IN THE WILD, **GOLDFISH** CAN GROW TO BE MORE THAN A **FOOT LONG.**
(0.3 m)

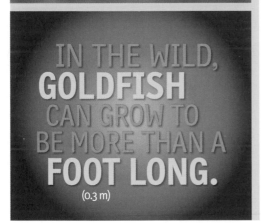

Locusts are a **popular snack** in parts of **Africa** and **Asia.**

SCANDINAVIANS IN **NORWAY** TRAVELED ON HANDMADE **SKIS** MORE THAN **6,000** YEARS AGO.

SCIENTISTS THINK THAT WATER ON THE MOON CAME FROM EARTH.

There's a road in New Jersey, U.S.A., named "Shades of Death."

A **CYCLIST INVENTED** A **BIKE HELMET** MADE FROM **RECYCLED NEWSPAPERS.**

AFRICAN LIONS
CATCH ABOUT
25 PERCENT
OF THE PREY
THEY CHASE.

25%

DRAGONFLIES
CATCH
95 PERCENT.

95%

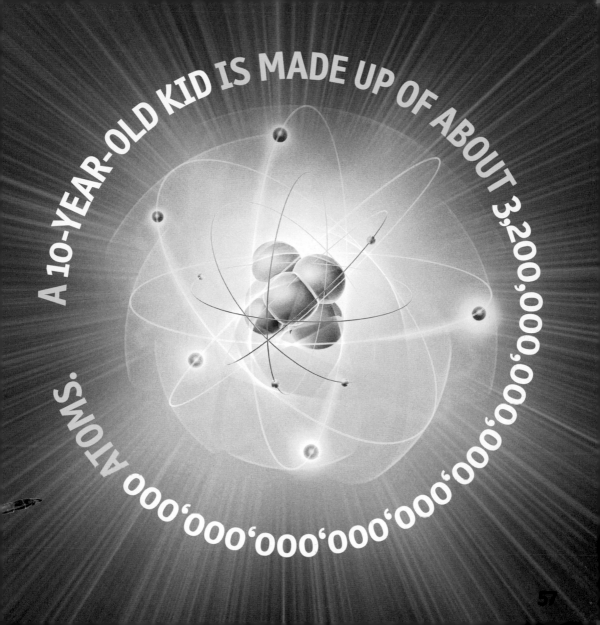

A 10-YEAR-OLD KID IS MADE UP OF ABOUT 3,200,000,000,000,000,000,000,000,000 ATOMS.

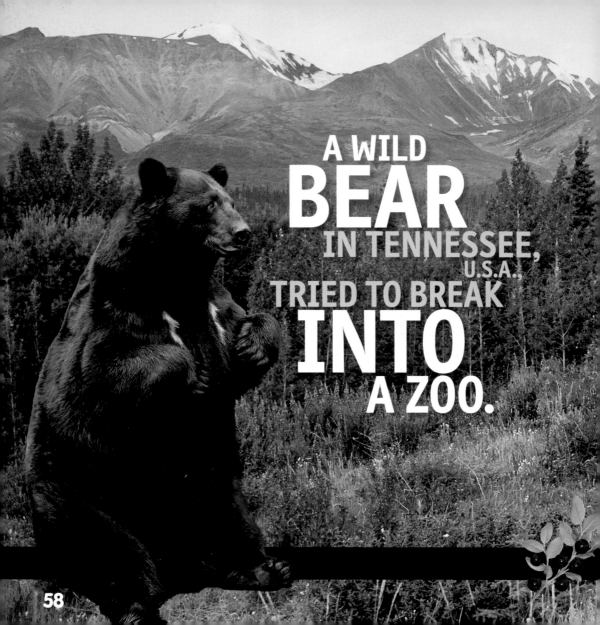

A WILD **BEAR** IN TENNESSEE, U.S.A., TRIED TO BREAK **INTO** A ZOO.

BEARS do not go to the BATHROOM for months while they're HIBERNATING.

THERE IS ABOUT ONE BEAR FOR EVERY TWO PEOPLE IN THE YUKON TERRITORY, CANADA.

A GRIZZLY BEAR CAN SNIFF OUT FOOD 18 MILES (29 km) AWAY.

Electric taxis
cruised the streets of
New York City **100**
more than
years ago.

New Zealand
has more
cats
per person
than any other
country in the
world.

A JAPANESE ARTIST
MAKES **SHELLS**
FOR **HERMIT CRABS**
THAT LOOK LIKE
CITY SKYLINES.

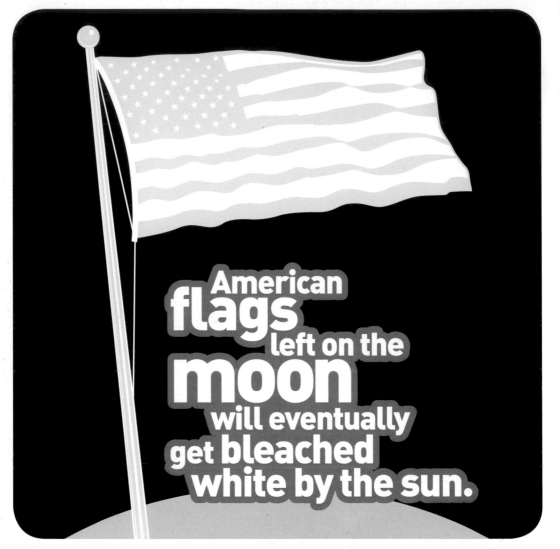

American **flags** left on the **moon** will eventually get **bleached** white by the sun.

A *designer* created a glow-in-the-dark *wedding dress*

EAT HOG WORLD
ty gammon and chicken sorbet
with a crunchy canine biscuit
nd served in a cone.
INE COOKIE CRUNCH
cious doggie delight of mixed dog
ts and ice cream topped with a
bone. Served in a traditional ice
cone.
free to donate 99p

AN ICE-CREAM TRUCK IN LONDON SERVED SCOOPS JUST FOR DOGS.

IT DOESN'T RAIN IN THE EYE OF A HURRICANE

A turtle's shell is made up of about 50 bones.

impossible hum your nose.

Atlantic lobsters sometimes eat each other.

A PICTURE PAINTED BY A RETIRED **RACEHORSE SOLD** FOR MORE THAN $2,000 ON eBAY.

A PALM TREE is not a tree; it's a type of GRASS.

NASCAR DRIVERS CAN TRAVEL THE LENGTH

OF A **FOOTBALL FIELD** IN JUST OVER A **SECOND.**

Some early **baseballs** were made of **fish eyes** covered in **leather.**

An **ELEPHANT'S skin** is as thick as **12 stacked PENNIES.**

A STUDY FOUND THAT **CHEESE** MAY TASTE **SALTIER EAT** IF YOU IT OFF A **KNIFE** INSTEAD OF A **FORK.**

STICK TO A FORK. IT'S SAFER!

SEAGULLS SOMETIMES SIT ON PELICANS' HEADS.

The White House, in Washington, D.C., U.S.A., was originally called the **President's Palace.**

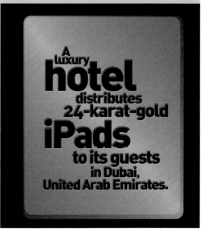

A luxury **hotel** distributes 24-karat-gold **iPads** to its guests in Dubai, United Arab Emirates.

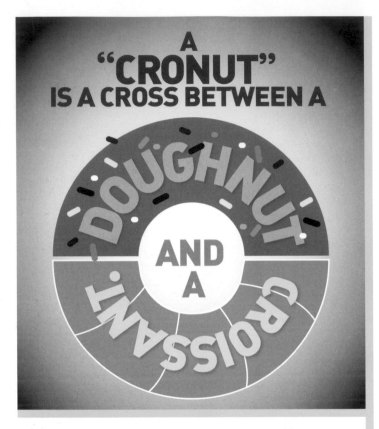

A **"CRONUT"** IS A CROSS BETWEEN A **DOUGHNUT** AND A **CROISSANT**

Amazon.com was originally called **"CADABRA."**

CHiMPANZEES CAN SWiM THE BREASTSTROKE.

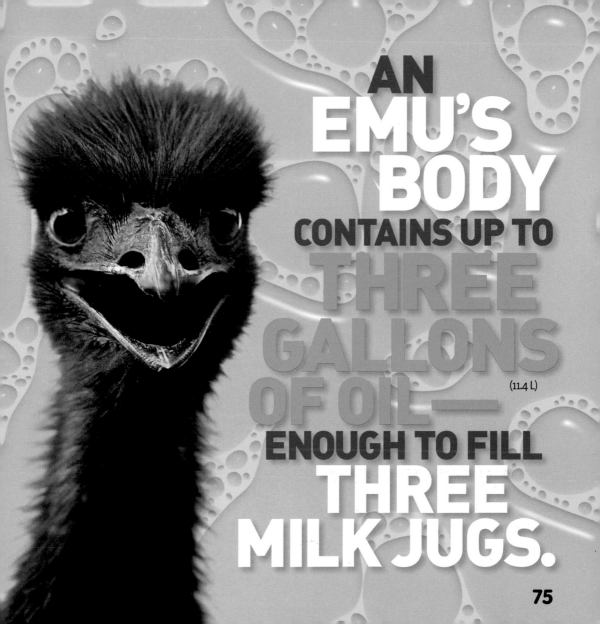

AN EMU'S BODY CONTAINS UP TO THREE GALLONS OF OIL— (11.4 L) ENOUGH TO FILL THREE MILK JUGS.

75

1,360 OLYMPIC-SIZE SWIMMING POOLS COULD FIT

INTO THE **WORLD'S LARGEST BUILDING,** LOCATED IN CHINA.

YOU LOSE ABOUT A MILLION SKIN CELLS EVERY 24 HOURS.

The first-ever webcam was used to watch a pot of coffee.

A FOUR-YEAR-OLD GIRL NAMED **DAISY** FOUND THE **BONE** OF A NEW **DINOSAUR** SPECIES, LATER NAMED *VECTIDRACO DAISYMORRISAE.*

Nosewise, Sturdy, and Hardy
were popular names
for *dogs* in
medieval times.

SOME MOTHS' HEARING IS
15 TIMES MORE SENSITIVE
THAN A HUMAN'S.

Muscles make up about **half** your body weight.

The **COOKIECUTTER SHARK** is named for the **COOKIE-SHAPED WOUNDS** it leaves in its **PREY.**

YOU CAN BUY **CANDY** THAT YOU CAN DRINK FROM A MINI– **TOILET BOWL.**

STEP ONE: POUR IN CANDY

STEP TWO: STIR

STEP THREE: DRINK!

Giant kelp can grow up to two feet in a day. (0.6 m)

You can get a massage 20 feet (6 m) under the sea in the world's first submarine spa.

A **DRAWING**
BY LEONARDO
DA VINCI—
A FAMOUS 15TH-CENTURY
ARTIST AND INVENTOR—
INSPIRED THE DESIGN
OF BATMAN'S
CAPE.

MUSICIANS
RE-CREATED THE
BATMAN
THEME SONG
USING REAL
BAT SOUNDS.

THERE'S AN AIRPORT IN TURKEY NAMED BATMAN.

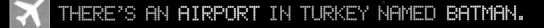

THE ORIGINAL **BATMOBILE** FROM THE 1960s *BATMAN* TV SHOW SOLD FOR **$4.2 MILLION.**

SOME **FISH** USE THEIR **FINS** **TO WALK** ALONG THE OCEAN FLOOR.

The world's **biggest** passenger **jet** weighs as much as **100 hippos.**

Pac-Man's shape was inspired by a whole pizza with a slice removed.

BALD PEOPLE ACTUALLY HAVE MICROSCOPIC HAIRS ON THEIR HEADS.

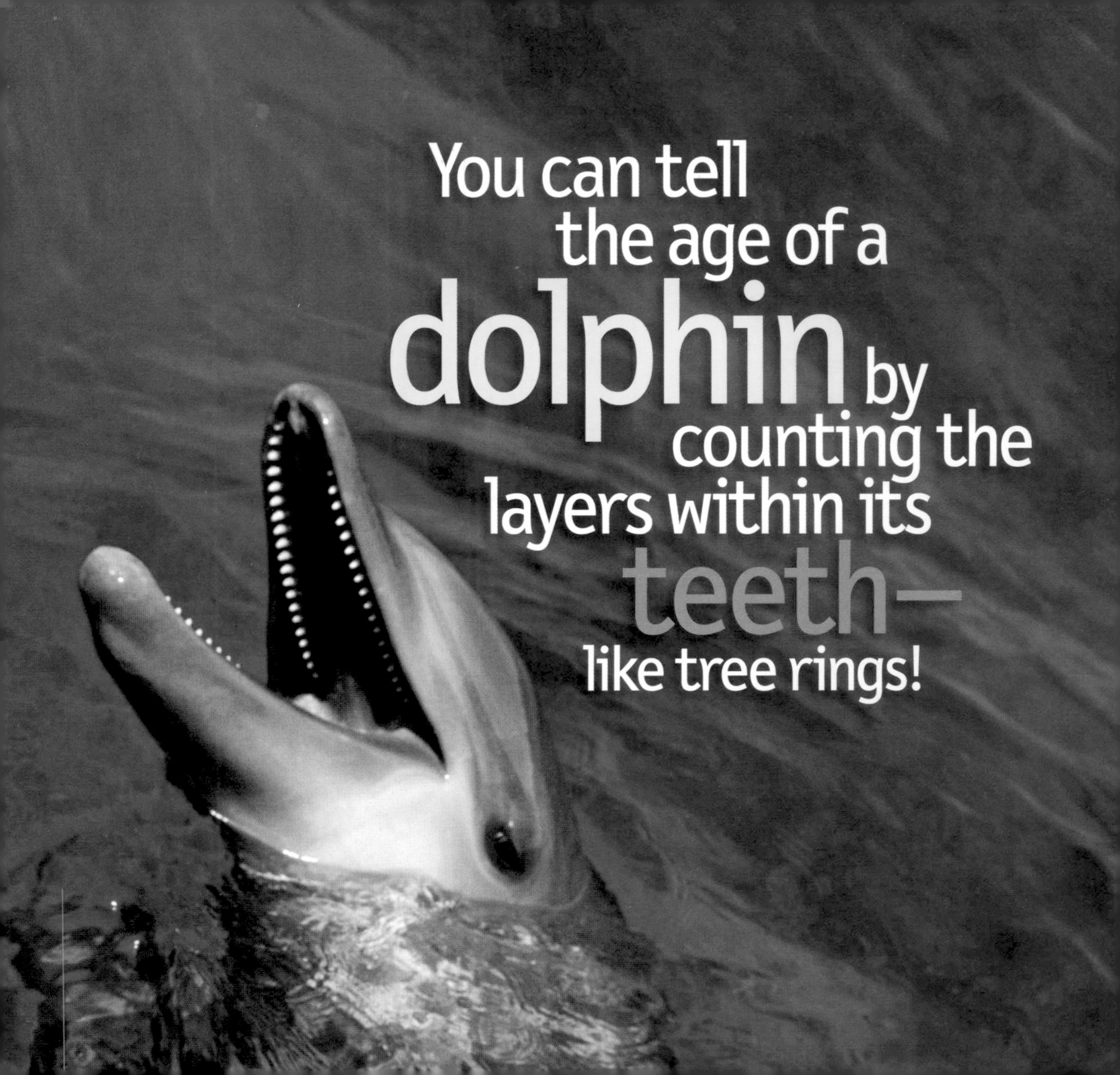

You can tell the age of a **dolphin** by counting the layers within its **teeth**— like tree rings!

DOLPHINS CAN **RECOGNIZE** AN OLD FRIEND'S WHISTLE, EVEN AFTER THEY'VE BEEN SEPARATED FOR 20 YEARS.

Mantises can remain alive without moving their heads.

THERE'S A MONUMENT DEDICATED TO THE BOLL WEEVIL BUG IN ALABAMA, U.S.A.

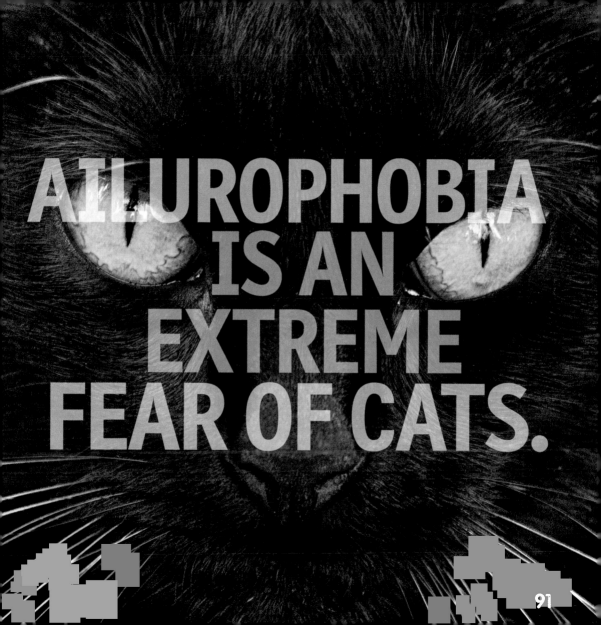

AILUROPHOBIA IS AN EXTREME FEAR OF CATS.

Geckos communicate by barking, chirping, and squeaking.

Shrimp swim BACKWARD.

Three out of four people admitted to sharing an ice-cream cone **with their pet,** a survey found.

Flatworms can regrow their heads.

More than **200 million emails are sent every minute** *on Earth.*

A **PRISON** IN **BRAZIL** **USES GEESE** AS AN ALARM SYSTEM— THEY HONK AT ANYONE ROAMING THE GROUNDS!

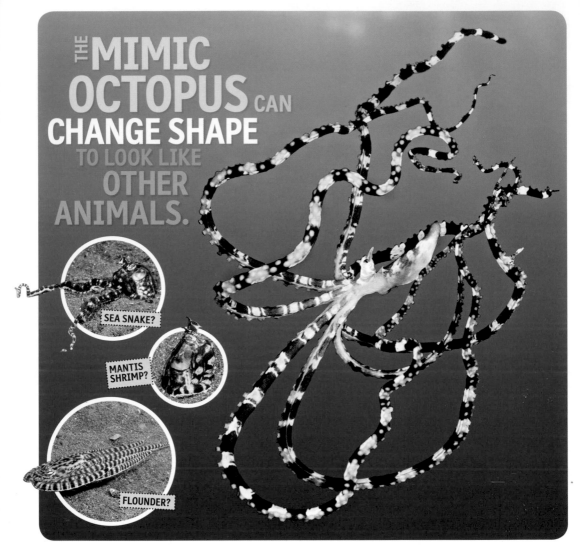

THE **MIMIC OCTOPUS** CAN **CHANGE SHAPE** TO LOOK LIKE **OTHER ANIMALS.**

SEA SNAKE?

MANTIS SHRIMP?

FLOUNDER?

THE INTERNATIONAL **SPACE STATION** IS THE MOST **EXPENSIVE** OBJECT EVER CONSTRUCTED-- COSTING SOME **$130 BILLION** TO BUILD.

HUNDREDS OF YEARS AGO, **RUSSIANS** BUILT THE FIRST **ROLLER COASTERS** FROM **ICE.**

The world's fastest **runner** generates enough energy in a 100-meter (328-foot) sprint **to power a vacuum.**

There's a **frog** that hears through its **mouth.**

THAT'S WEIRD!

CORN FLAKES CEREAL was first served in a hospital as an easy-to-digest food.

You have **taste buds** in your **throat.**

A woman once made a **whoopie pie** weighing **1,062 pounds—** (482 kg) enough for **6,000 servings.**

BAKED CATERPILLARS TASTE LIKE PISTACHIOS.

DON'T TRY THIS AT HOME!

The
blue whale—
the largest animal
on Earth—can't
swallow anything
bigger than a
beach ball.

BLUE WHALE CALVES GAIN 9 POUNDS (4 kg) PER HOUR

BLUE WHALES DO UNDERWATER BARREL ROLLS BEFORE CATCHING PREY.

FOR THE FIRST SEVEN MONTHS OF THEIR LIVES.

STUDIES SHOW THAT THE AVERAGE DAYDREAM IS ABOUT 14 SECONDS LONG.

Male pandas sometimes do handstands to mark trees.

For $25, you can order a **jar of human toenails online.**

THE SPEED OF LIGHT IS 18 MILLION TIMES FASTER THAN THE SPEED OF RAIN.

The ***Kilauea volcano*** *on the Big Island of Hawaii, U.SA.,* *has been erupting for* ***30 years.***

Before it hit stores, **the iPhone was known as "Purple."**

SOME **BIRDS** HIBERNATE.

ORANGUTANS SOMETIMES MAKE **WHISTLES** OUT OF LEAVES.

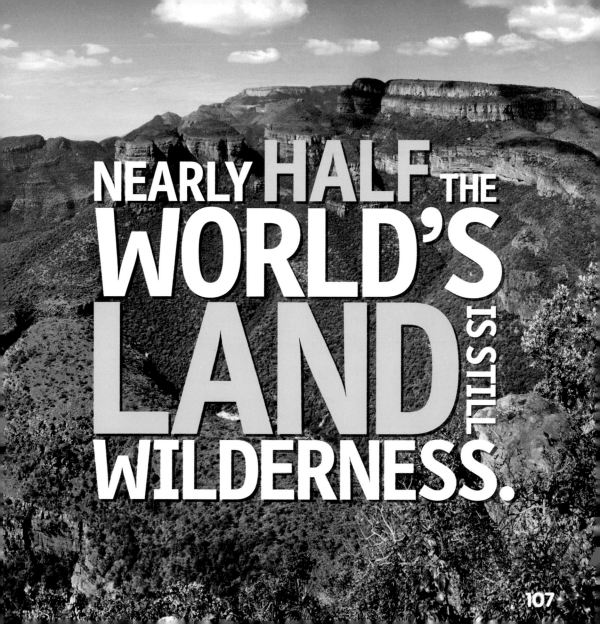

NEARLY HALF THE WORLD'S LAND IS STILL WILDERNESS.

100 billion servings of **instant ramen noodles** are **sold every year.**

(That's 14 bowls for every person on Earth!)

EVERY YEAR, RESIDENTS IN A NEW MEXICO, U.S.A., TOWN **BUILD A GIANT SNOWMAN** OUT OF **TUMBLEWEEDS.**

The longest unbroken apple peel was as long as an Olympic-size pool.

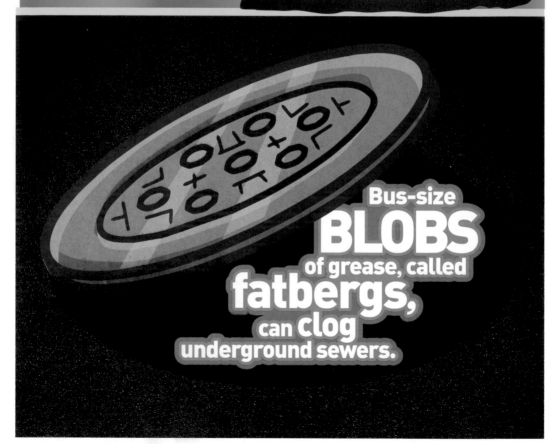

Bus-size **BLOBS** of grease, called **fatbergs,** can **clog** underground sewers.

A restaurant in Singapore once sold a **pizza within a pizza.**

Some beetles' bellies glow orange.

When threatened, a copperhead snake releases musk that smells like **cucumbers.**

STORM SYSTEMS IN THE SKY CAN HOLD **MORE WATER** THAN THE **MISSISSIPPI RIVER.**

IT TOOK **ARTISTS** SOME **17,000 HOURS** TO BUILD A **LIFE-SIZE STAR WARS X-WING STARFIGHTER** ENTIRELY FROM **LEGOS.**

THE FURRY CHEWBACCA BAT IS NAMED AFTER THE STAR WARS CHARACTER.

A FAST FOOD RESTAURANT IN FRANCE OFFERS DARTH VADER BURGERS WITH BUNS THAT ARE DYED BLACK.

Perfectly preserved honey has been found in ancient Egyptian tombs.

IT WOULD TAKE 225 MILLION YEARS TO WALK A LIGHT-YEAR.

You can order deep-fried jelly beans at some state fairs.

There
are only
two sets of
escalators in
the entire state
of Wyoming, U.S.A.

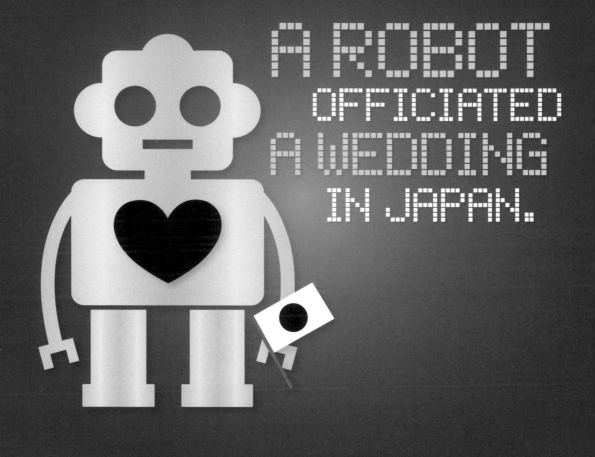

A ROBOT OFFICIATED A WEDDING IN JAPAN.

Redheads
in Australia
are sometimes
called
"Blueys."

The **meteorite** that most likely **killed** off the **dinosaurs** was the size of San Francisco, California, U.S.A.

Donald Duck's middle name is FAUNTLEROY.

THE
OARFISH
CAN
GROW
TO BE
LONGER
THAN A
SCHOOL
BUS.

A flawless pink diamond
was auctioned for
$83 million.

SOME
ZOO
ANIMALS
SNACK ON
"BLOODSICLES"
TO STAY
COOL
DURING
HEAT WAVES.

Choir members' **heartbeats sync** when they **sing,** a study found.

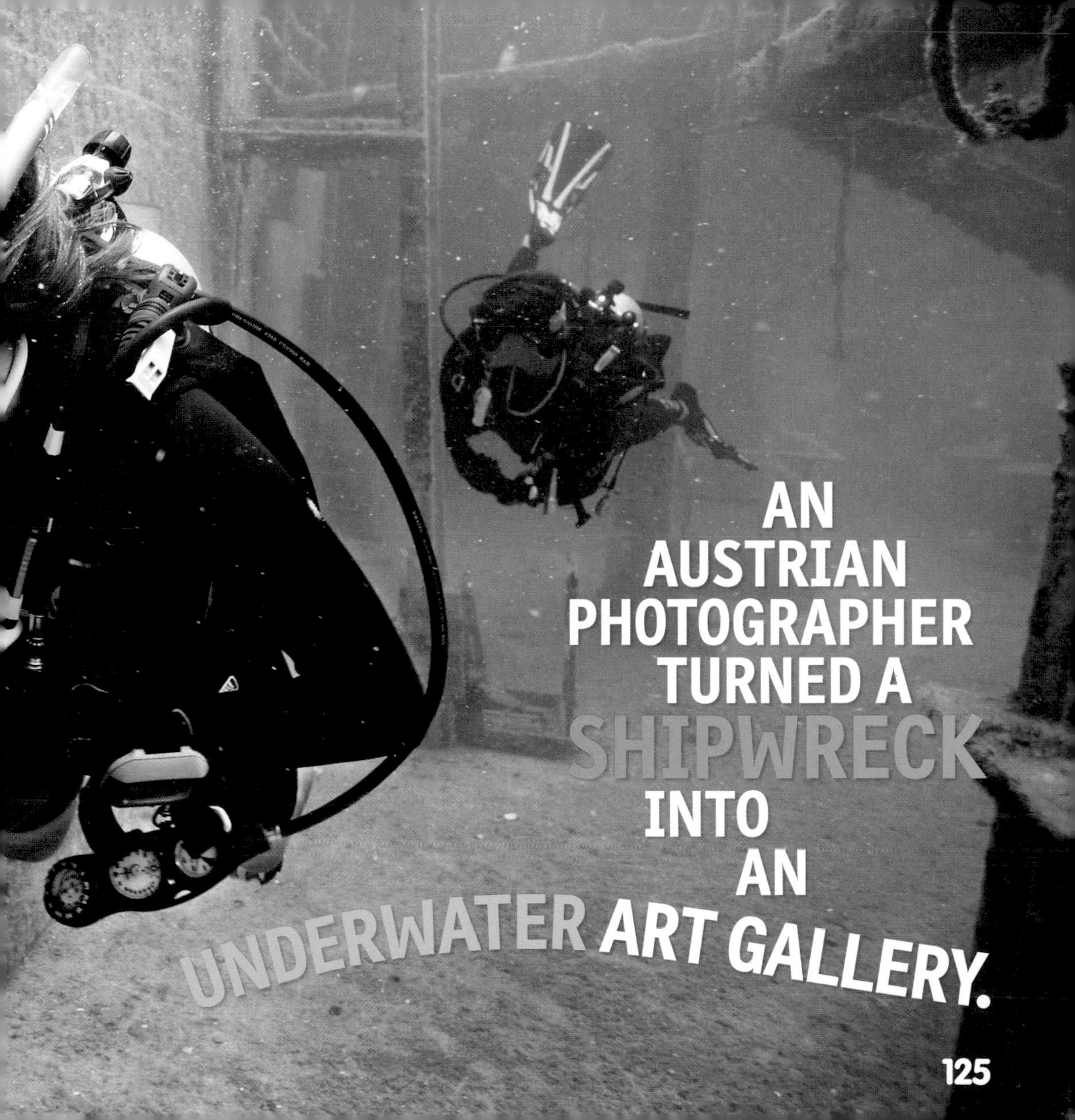

AN
AUSTRIAN
PHOTOGRAPHER
TURNED A
SHIPWRECK
INTO
AN
UNDERWATER ART GALLERY.

A **ZOO** in England banned visitors from wearing **animal print clothes** to avoid confusing the wildlife.

IT TAKES ABOUT THE SAME AMOUNT OF **force** TO PULL YOUR FOOT OUT OF **quicksand** AS IT DOES TO **lift a car.**

Soccer's World Cup trophy is worth about $250,000!

There's a **world snail racing championship** held in England **every year.**

#23

Buttered toast almost always falls butter-side down.

THE LION'S MANE
JELLYFISH
CAN GROW TO
BE LONGER THAN
SEVEN SUVs.

THE CITY OF **AMSTERDAM,** IN THE NETHERLANDS, HAS MORE **BIKES** THAN PEOPLE.

CATS AND DOGS CAN GET SUNBURNED.

Belgian chocolate

BELGIE-BELGIQUE

In **Belgium,**
there are
postage stamps
that smell and taste
like chocolate.

ONE ARGENTINIAN
ARTIST
CREATES IMAGES BY
SHOOTING PAINT
OUT OF HIS EYE
ONTO CANVAS.

SOME LIZARDS HAVE GREEN BONES.

The *Caloplaca obamae* fungus is named after President Obama.

You can cook **fish** in your **dishwasher.**

A 16-YEAR-OLD **CHEERLEADER** LANDED IN THE RECORD BOOKS AFTER DOING **40 BACKFLIPS** IN A ROW.

People tend to **sleep less** when there's a **FULL MOON.**

Voyager 1 is the first spacecraft to leave the solar system—more than 11 billion miles from Earth.

(17,702,784,000 km)

Mistletoe *has no* **scent.**

420 million years ago, mushrooms grew taller than giraffes.

A MANHATTAN **PIZZERIA** SELLS A **12-INCH** (31-cm) **PIZZA** WITH CAVIAR TOPPING FOR **$1,000.**

There are **rivers** on one of Saturn's **moons.**

SOME RATS ARE TRAINED TO SNIFF OUT BOMBS.

You can buy cola-flavored Cheetos in Japan.

About half the people ON EARTH live in an area where SNOW never falls.

Parrotfish sleep in a bag of their own MUCUS.

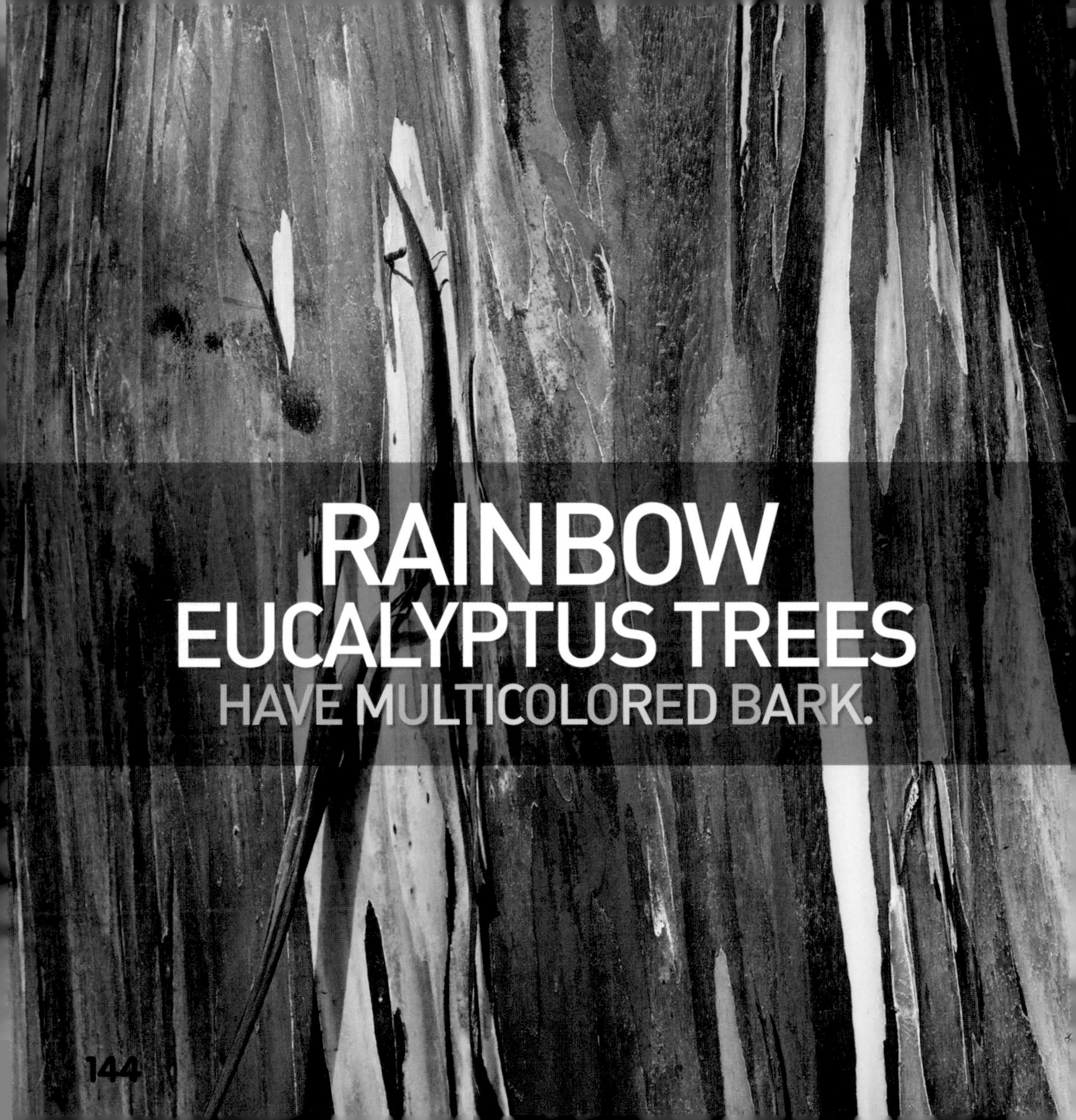

RAINBOW
EUCALYPTUS TREES
HAVE MULTICOLORED BARK.

A tiny park in Oregon, U.S.A., is smaller than a skateboard.

A WOMAN IN FLORIDA, U.S.A., FOUND A STRAWBERRY SHAPED LIKE A GRIZZLY BEAR.

There's a machine that turns sweat into drinking water.

The first Tweet from Google read "I'm 01100110 01100101 01100101 01101100 01101001 01101110 01100111 00100000 01101100 01111010 01101001 01101011 01111001 00001010."

SCOOBY-DOO
WAS ORIGINALLY NAMED
TOO MUCH.

147

TIGERS AND HOUSE CATS

SHARE 95 PERCENT OF THE SAME GENES.

Northern Spy, Wealthy, and Twenty Ounce are all types of **apples.**

Hundreds of years ago,
**people played tennis
with their bare hands**
—no racquet required!

King cobras can grow as **long** as a giraffe is tall.

THERE MAY BE **100 TIMES** MORE WATER BENEATH **AFRICA** THAN ON ITS SURFACE.

Of the **1,100 species of bats,** only **two walk** on the ground.

AN EXTINCT **VOLCANO** THE SIZE OF **ITALY** LIES UNDERNEATH THE **PACIFIC OCEAN.**

AN OLYMPIC WRESTLING MATCH ONCE LASTED 11 HOURS.

CHIHUAHUA + **DACHSHUND**

CHIWEENIE

You can mail a postcard from AUSTRALIA'S Great Barrier Reef—45 miles from shore. (72 km)

SOME **FISH** CAN **GROW** ALMOST A **QUARTER OF THEIR BODY LENGTH** IN A SINGLE DAY.

Earth **bulges** at the Equator.

It would take the strength of five people to "tip" a standing cow.

HELLO
my name is

THE BIRD ON THE TWITTER LOGO IS NAMED LARRY.

SCOLIONOPHOBIA IS A FEAR OF SCHOOL.

HORSERADISH IS A MEMBER OF THE MUSTARD FAMILY.

SEVERAL SHIPS ARE BURIED

UNDER BUILDINGS

IN SAN FRANCISCO, CALIFORNIA, U.S.A.

PEOPLE WAITED IN A 7-MILE LINE TO EAT AT THE FIRST-EVER MCDONALD'S IN KUWAIT.

(11 km)

Today's cell phones are more POWERFUL than the computers that sent ASTRONAUTS to the MOON.

Alaska is the **northernmost,** **westernmost,** and *easternmost* **state** in the **United States.**

AVOCADOS ARE TOXIC TO MOST BIRDS.

THE SHORTEST COMMERCIAL FLIGHT IS JUST TWO MINUTES LONG.

"Watermelon snow"
IS TINTED PINK AND SMELLS SWEET.

SOME BUTTERFLIES DRINK TURTLE TEARS.

AMERICANS BUY SOME **THREE** (4,828,032 km) **MILLION MILES** OF DENTAL FLOSS EVERY YEAR.

Vinegar can dissolve pearls.

DON'T TRY THIS AT HOME!

WHEN THREATENED, THE HELLBENDER SALAMANDER, ALSO CALLED A SNOT OTTER, OOZES CLEAR SLIME.

Gorillas sleep in nests.

You spend about an hour a day CHEWING.

ALL **CLOWNFISH** ARE BORN **MALE.**

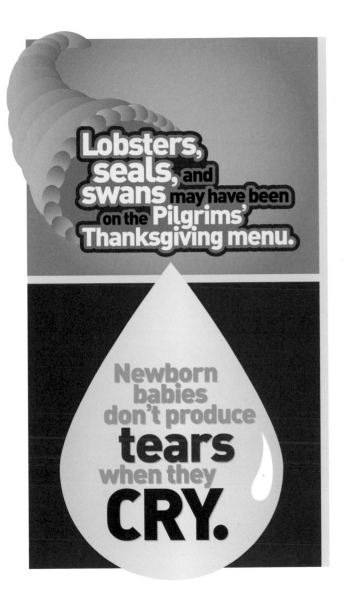

Lobsters, seals, and swans may have been on the **Pilgrims'** Thanksgiving menu.

Newborn babies don't produce **tears** when they **CRY.**

THE **EYE** OF A HURRICANE ON **SATURN** IS SO HUGE, IT WOULD **STRETCH** FROM **LONDON,** ENGLAND, TO MOSCOW, **RUSSIA.**

Thousands of brand-new **sneakers** once washed ashore on a Dutch island.

Some astronauts
train for space walks
by walking on the
OCEAN FLOOR.

Giant **CLAMS** can grow AS LONG AS **two** skateboards.

Kiwifruits were originally called "melonettes."

A MAN FLOATED FOR **235 MILES** (378 km) IN A **CHAIR** TIED TO MORE THAN **150** HELIUM **BALLOONS.**

THE SOUND
OF AN
ICEBERG
BREAKING
IS LOUDER THAN
214 OIL TANKER
ENGINES.

A FISHERMAN NEAR NORWAY REELED IN A 9-FOOT-LONG (2.7-m) HALIBUT THAT WEIGHED MORE THAN A GORILLA.

It is a crime to wear jeans in North Korea.

MORE THAN 30 MILLION PEOPLE IN CHINA LIVE IN CAVES.

PIGEONS
CAN RECOGNIZE
THEMSELVES
IN A MIRROR.

An **alligator** loses and regrows **teeth** up to **50** times during its lifetime.

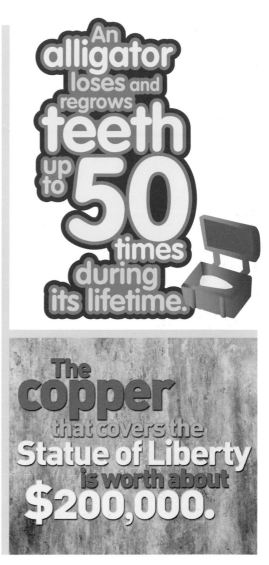

The **copper** that covers the **Statue of Liberty** is worth about **$200,000.**

A whale's
EARWAX
can be as thick as a
mattress.

You can **stay**
IN A
luxury cave
at an **inn** in
NEW MEXICO, U.S.A.

SCIENTISTS THINK
THAT IT RAINS
GLASS ON
SOME PLANETS.

THERE ARE
NO SEAGULLS
IN HAWAII, U.S.A.

ASH FROM
VOLCANIC ERUPTIONS
CAN MAKE THE
MOON LOOK
BLUE FROM EARTH.

Snub-nosed
monkeys
sneeze
when it rains.

EIGHT COLLEGE FOOTBALL PLAYERS COMPETED AGAINST TWO ASIAN ELEPHANTS IN A **WATERMELON-EATING** CONTEST.

(THE HUMANS LOST.)

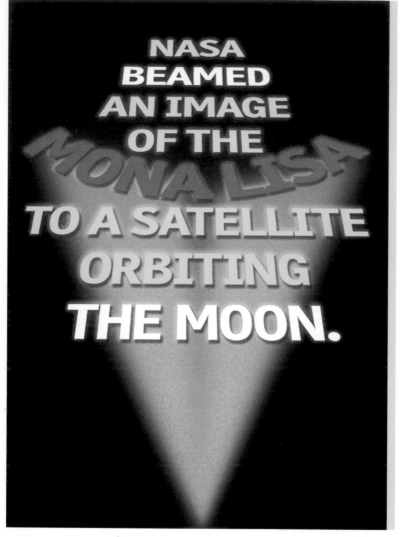

NASA BEAMED AN IMAGE OF THE MONA LISA TO A SATELLITE ORBITING THE MOON.

PREHISTORIC PEOPLE USED "SUPERGLUE" MADE FROM TREE SAP AND PIGMENT SOME 70,000 YEARS AGO.

THE AVERAGE AMERICAN USES MORE THAN 20,000 SQUARES OF TOILET PAPER IN A YEAR.

THERE ARE ABOUT **300 DIMPLES** ON A **GOLF BALL.**

Horseshoe crabs have powder blue blood.

THE THINNEST GLASS IN THE WORLD IS 20-BILLIONTHS OF AN INCH (2.5 CM) THICK.

Some **pigs** have **curly hair.**

Music broadcast from the **International Space Station** played over the radio **on Earth.**

SOME MOTH COCOONS CAN BE USED TO MAKE PURSES.

SOME FISH CAN **TASTE** WITH THEIR TAILS.

The scientific name for **brain freeze** is *sphenopalatine ganglioneuralgia.*

CHIPMUNKS **see** in *slow motion.*

189

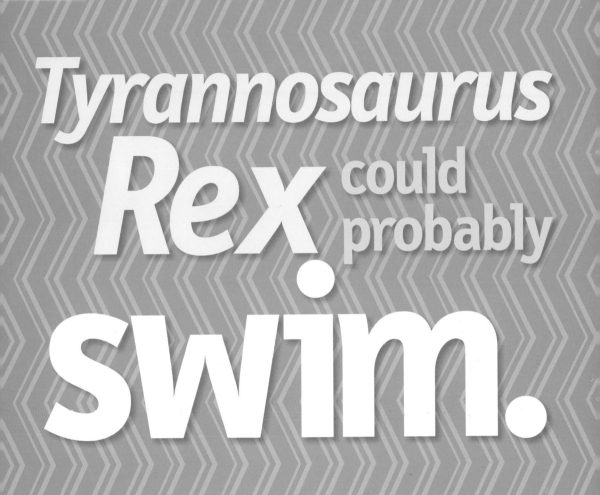

Tyrannosaurus
Rex. could
probably
swim.

THERE'S A **HOTEL** WITH **GUEST ROOMS** MADE OUT OF OLD **DRAINAGE PIPES.**

january

february

march

april

may

august

cember

Large **crocodiles** can survive for more than a year without eating.

THERE ARE MORE THAN **1,900 EDIBLE INSECT SPECIES** ON EARTH.

THERE'S A BAND THAT PLAYS INSTRUMENTS MADE FROM OLD CAR PARTS.

THE "STRUTBONE" IS MADE FROM THE STRUTS OF A CAR!

ATHLETES ATE CHEESECAKE DURING THE FIRST OLYMPIC GAMES IN GREECE.

Flying vampire **frogs** have **black fangs** when they are **tadpoles.**

Lipstick-wearers who lick their **lips** can eat up to two spoonfuls of makeup a year.

YOU HAVE ABOUT **FOUR MILLION** SWEAT GLANDS IN YOUR BODY.

There's a
pink lake
in Australia.

A NEW TYPE OF **WETSUIT** CAMOUFLAGES

SURFERS SO SHARKS CAN'T SEE THEM.

Scientists think **sharks** are color-blind.

FACTFINDER

Illustrations are indicated by **boldface.**

FACTFINDER

FACTFINDER

PHOTO CREDITS

Published by the National Geographic Society
John M. Fahey, *Chairman of the Board and Chief Executive Officer*
Declan Moore, *Executive Vice President; President, Publishing and Travel*
Melina Gerosa Bellows, *Publisher, Chief Creative Officer, Books, Kids, and Family*

Prepared by the Book Division
Hector Sierra, *Senior Vice President and General Manager*
Nancy Laties Feresten, *Senior Vice President, Kids Publishing and Media*
Jennifer Emmett, *Vice President, Editorial Director, Kids Books*
Eva Absher-Schantz, *Design Director, Kids Publishing and Media*
Jay Sumner, *Director of Photography, Kids Publishing*
R. Gary Colbert, *Production Director*
Jennifer A. Thornton, *Director of Managing Editorial*

Staff for This Book
Robin Terry, Ariane Szu-Tu, *Project Editors*
Eva Absher-Schantz, *Art Director*
Rachael Hamm Plett, Moduza Design, *Designer*
Hillary Leo, *Associate Photo Editor*
Julie Beer, Michelle Harris, *Researchers*
Callie Broaddus, *Design Production Assistant*
Margaret Leist, *Photo Assistant*
Grace Hill, *Associate Managing Editor*
Joan Gossett, *Production Editor*
Lewis R. Bassford, *Production Manager*
Susan Borke, *Legal and Business Affairs*
Paige Towler, *Editorial Intern*

Based on the "Weird But True" department in *National Geographic Kids* magazine

Production Services
Phillip L. Schlosser, *Senior Vice President*
Chris Brown, *Vice President, Book Manufacturing*
George Bounelis, *Senior Production Manager*
Nicole Elliott, *Director of Production*
Rachel Faulise, *Manager*
Robert L. Barr, *Manager*
Darrick McRae, *Imaging Technician*

Wanna hear something weird but NOT true?

EATING CHOCOLATE GIVES YOU PIMPLES.

ORIGIN
This idea has been around for nearly a century, and cultures around the world believe diet can affect skin health.

80

WRONG! No proof, so munch away (in moderation of course)!

Find out the real deal on more than 100 **tall tales**, **curious claims**, **suspicious stories**, and **unbelievable urban legends!**

Bet you'll also like

AVAILABLE WHEREVER BOOKS ARE SOLD